IN PLAIN SIGHT HIDDEN
POEMS FROM A TIN CAN PILGRIM

LYNDA ROZELL

ST. BONA'S PRESS

Copyright © 2022 Lynda Rozell

Text and Photographs by Lynda Rozell

Cover Design by St. Bona's Press

All rights reserved

ISBN: 979-8-9857458-1-8

ST. BONA'S PRESS

Published by St. Bona's Press
www.stbonaspress.com
Contact info@stbonaspress.com
for bulk orders at retail or wholesale

FOR MY DAUGHTERS

CONTENTS

Introduction and Thanks   i

Part One: Nature

Lily Pads   2

After the Storm   5

By the Shore of the Lake   8

Feather   10

Mosquitoes in Heaven   14

Part Two: Camping

Airstream Rally Reverie   18

Balloon Fiesta in Silver   23

Tomatoes and Tornadoes   27

Fireside   31

Storms and Inner Peace   34

Part Three: Identity

The Gardener   38

A Gentle Conversation on My Drive North   42

Friends Now and Forever	47
Spiritual Childhood	50
Your Dwelling Place	53

Part Four: God

By the Side of the River	58
Walking with Jesus at the Shore	60
With my Friend in Prayer and Work	62

Part Five: Prayer

A Pilgrim's Prayer	68
A Prayer for Trust	70
All for Love	73
About the Author	75

INTRODUCTION

I live in a tin can — an Airstream travel trailer. As a full-time nomad, I explore parks, religious sites, and areas of incredible natural beauty in the United States.

Last year, I wrote about how I left a traditional life with a corporate job in an urban environment to become a wandering pilgrim. My book *Journeys with a Tin Can Pilgrim: from corporate lawyer to Airstream nomad, finding joy in everyday life* tells stories about how I found my true identity, discovered Airstreams and their heritage, learned how to live in and tow a recreational vehicle (RV), and engaged with communities on the road. More than a "how to RV" manual, my first book invites readers into a relationship with their Creator, interweaving Scripture and reflections with life on the road.

This new book uses poetry to further explore how living close to nature inspires creativity and connection with God. We become more like our Creator the more we create, inspired by the beauty of His Creation. For me, that means rediscovering a childhood hobby of writing poetry. I've also learned more about photography. Each poem has a few introductory words and some a photograph, as a way to give context for the poem.

The first part of this collection addresses nature and the beauty of Creation. The next part explores camping — the place where I find connection with nature and others, especially God. Meditations about identity and relationship comprise the third part of this poetry collection, leading to contemplation of God in the fourth part. Last, I conclude with prayer rooted in all that went before.

Thank you to all who heard and commented on my draft poems in campgrounds, restaurants, and coffee bars. Also, thanks in particular to Laura Ruberto, Rose Folsom, and Father Jerry Wooton for their insightful feedback.

I hope that these poems may inspire you in your search for who you are, who God is, and your relationship with Him. In some way, each poem reflects my delight in the beauty of nature, the love of God for all, and the desire to be close to Him. May they leave you with a smile and an uplifted heart!

PART ONE: NATURE

LILY PADS

God speaks to us in the beauty of small details of nature as well as in the vast panoramas of shore and sky. Lily pads floating on the surface of a little pond caught my attention recently as I walked through a crowded park. Sometimes we need to remember to stop and look to see beyond the surface.

I wander by a still deep pond

Small bridges frame its edges

And as I stop and look, I see

A masterpiece, a ballet

A painting come alive for me

The inspiration of Monet

Lily pads shimmer on the water

Glimmer in the light

Circles missing a slice

Slight puckery leaves

muted not bright

Varied shades of saffron,

Some with silver glazed brown

A gathering of every green

IN PLAIN SIGHT HIDDEN

There, almost a purple sheen

With buds, no blossoms yet

Leaves like artists' palettes

Float gently in still water

Form abstract shapes in touching one another

I step closer now to the still deep pond

Tread lightly on the small inviting bridges

camera in hand seeking to select

a still life painted without brushes

Whole worlds live in each lily pad

Framed with reeds and rushes

The pond a universe of sky and trees

The pads a sumptuous soft shroud

Dragonflies hover without any breeze

No-see-ums rise in a cloud

Yet the lily pads simply float content

on the surface beneath the sky

IN PLAIN SIGHT HIDDEN

the border between what lies above

and what hides beneath as I pass by

Their soft colors form a symphony

of hues that blend harmoniously

A visual melody

Spun on the water

Sung under the sky

I cannot capture with my lens

The glory that it magnifies

A masterpiece that signifies

The Creator's love that underlies

All that we are given

Seen and unseen

Before our eyes

In plain sight hidden

As we pass by

AFTER THE STORM

The ocean fascinates me with how it changes. After a storm, the beach contains all sorts of debris tossed by high tides. At Topsail Hill State Preserve in Florida, collapsed bright blue Portuguese Men O' War dotted the white sand amid splintered bark and sticks following a windy overnight downpour. Here's a glimpse into that moment.

    Today like glass or the surface of a precious marble flattened

    swirls of color and faint tracks of bird feet

    mark the revealed smooth layers leading to the water's edge

    Yesterday's sand-blasted bright blue balloons

    Lie twisted and grayed along the edges of the tidal line

    Cast out and up

    Other colorful deadly bubbles drained far out into the gulf

    Past the smooth sand the tide revealed

    leading to the water's edge

IN PLAIN SIGHT HIDDEN

We walked and talked

now that the breeze no longer snatched our words away

As the skittering terns skipped forward, back, then returned

Along the glistening smooth sand

leading to the water's edge

And we left behind loss and lethargy

swaddled but trapped in warm blankets now unwrapped

scoured clean by the sand and spray

And with the storm's remnants gently washed away

Fading in the gentle light filtered through the clouds

smoothing the sand like glass

leading to the water's edge.

IN PLAIN SIGHT HIDDEN

BY THE SHORE OF THE LAKE

Early one morning I walked along a trail by a still lake. The trees and sky appeared upside down in its waters. In a seemingly peaceful scene, I spotted a man fishing by the shore in waders. As I drew closer, I could see something moving in the grass near him. It was a large fish, frantically flopping, trying to get back to the water.

Like and unlike

Bubbles, striations, swirls like air trapped in panes of old glass

A world upside down that wavers and bends

A dream, an echo of reality

Or perhaps I wait in the dreamworld

where straight trunks, sharp edged rocks,

echoes of branches

slice the sun into pieces that sparkle on still glass

Plop!

A fish jumps, breaking my reverie

and spilling the upside-down world into circles widening

IN PLAIN SIGHT HIDDEN

Destroyer of worlds

Slimy finned one

You touch the line that bends upon entering the mirror

Glass shatters as you frantically seek escape

Snagged by reality, drawn up into the world of air

Gasping

At the loss of your deep dreams below

Iridescence plays on your skin while fathomless eyes stare

Stillness breaks into flapping

no longer graceful but the subject of grace

before meals

Your beauty fades

For a new delectable appearance as you sizzle on the grill

White flesh steaming when my fork breaks your skin

Now part of this world devouring you

Destroyer of worlds

Now restored

By your sacrifice

FEATHER

In winter I was hiking along the Gulf Shores of Florida admiring birds and the patterns of flowing water. Little terns darted back and forth chased by the waves. I spotted a small feather tangled up in a pile of shells and picked it up. Fascinated by the detail, I later rinsed it in water to more clearly see its construction and patterns. This poem ensued.

You float through the air

Soft fibers parting

Two speckles of white on a black tip

With grey beneath, glistening, darting

Fading to white in your slender center binding

Roots barely visible hook barbed branches finding

A tether at your spine like veins on a leaf

Anchors lines that run to the ends of each sheaf

How did you get here?

Did you fall, forced out by new growth,

Pushed out past your prime?

Did you launch yourself from a passing trapeze,

IN PLAIN SIGHT HIDDEN

Defying your short time

Soaring, spiraling in slow descent

To the shore below?

Freed from your source, riding the breeze,

Not realizing how far you'd go.

 Did a hungry hawk strike, rend the wings you uplifted,

Break you apart from all you knew, shifted,

from hunter to prey?

Though diminished, you exist, you stay

No longer high above

but still recalling that glory from which you strayed

Fallen, shorn.

You cannot return

Like a quill pen at rest

You have stories to tell that you cannot say

Tongue-tied, silenced on the ground you stay

IN PLAIN SIGHT HIDDEN

You soar no more

No longer sprint from the spitting spray

Escape the reach of waves adorned

by plumes of frost white foam

No longer in formation joined, now lost and alone

You cannot run but are wrung out

Tumbling in these shifting sands

Scraping skin as you're tossed about

Brittle shells tangling your strands

I wrest you from their grasp

Scoop you up from the shelter you clasp

You thought yourself safe inside

But you were trapped, discarded, cast aside

Your softness reemerges as I rinse away

the smothering sticky sand

Free you from the grinding grains

IN PLAIN SIGHT HIDDEN

that grate against my hand

Splayed against my palm, your straggled fronds unstained

I stroke you gently, smooth your strands

trace my fingertips along your veins,

Slight but full of light regained;

Threads weave patterns in overlapping planes

Two speckles of white on a black tip

Above soft glistening gray

Your plumage paying homage still

To the breath of the living mystery

That restores to you such harmony

Much more than before your fall, fulfilled.

MOSQUITOES IN HEAVEN

I wrote this little poem in bad humor, annoyed by mosquitoes screaming in my ear and biting me. These pests often lead me to douse myself with bug spray when I emerge from my Airstream. In many countries, though, they are a far more serious problem, spreading terrible diseases. So, what was God thinking when He created mosquitoes? He has infinite patience even with small questions.

Are there mosquitoes in Heaven?

I should like to know

For I don't understand

Why they're here below

What purpose, dear Lord,

Do they serve in this world?

They bite, spread disease

Fly in mouths when we breathe

Sprinkle our skins with angry red bumps

Irritate livestock, clog water pumps

Sure, in swatting or shaking them away

IN PLAIN SIGHT HIDDEN

I may find some humor on a good day

As I canter, cavort, and contort to escape

Only to find them dive-bombing my face

Lord, I love you and know You're all wise

But why mosquitoes, why? Unlike flies

Who at least serve a purpose - promoting decay -

Mosquitoes exist it seems only to prey

On people and animals, until there's a freeze

Spreading illness, not pollen, unlike the bees

Pray tell, Lord, so I may know

Is there some blessing these whiners bestow?

Or are they just part of our fallen estate

Departed, distorted from an intended trait?

Did you mean them for music,

Or to create a sweet breeze,

Fanning the brows of Adam and Eve?

IN PLAIN SIGHT HIDDEN

Amusing our parents with fanciful swarms

Like small jewels scattered amid Eden's charms?

Of all, dear Lord, that has gone astray

Warped and corrupted from Eden's fair day

Mosquitoes cry out to be made new

Still, their torments may turn us toward you

As we offer our bites, scratches and stings

Sicknesses spread by these nasty small things

Like all pain and hurt suffered below

Redeemed by the cross, love from sorrow

And Lord, you don't owe an answer to me

Mosquitoes may remain a mystery

Until that day when we meet face to face

And no questions remain, all becomes grace

PART TWO: CAMPING

AIRSTREAM RALLY REVERIE

An Airstream rally is a gathering of Airstreams in one area, whether at a campground, on the streets of an accommodating small town, or in a fairground. They build community in a variety of ways from a maintenance rally in Delaware to the improvised social plans at the CanOpener Rally in Santa Rosa Beach, Florida. Each year hundreds of Airstreams converge for the Airstream International Rally. This event has something for everyone, from seminars on wine tasting and cooking to awning use, towing tips, and solar energy systems, along with plenty of shared meals and fun.

    One by one the silver bullets rumble in

    A Bambi, a Land Shark, Globetrotter, Safari

    Excella, Caravel, Classic, Serenity

    Now the Atlas, Interstate, and even Argosy

    Flying Clouds as far as the eye can see

    Scores of Airstreams tethered by bright cords

    To pedestals sprouting up from the ground

    Gathering the shiny tin can hordes

IN PLAIN SIGHT HIDDEN

All sizes and vintages, silver all around

Here to celebrate a community found

Airstreamers are a friendly crew

They warmly welcome anyone new

Need some help?

Can you see me in your mirror?

Pull straight, then cut your wheel toward me

You've got six feet to go, now three

Okay - stop or you'll hit that tree!

Reunions wait for unhitching

Then setting up your site

Stabilizer drills whirring

Fantastic fans twirling

Flags raising, wind chimes dancing

All sorts of flamingos prancing

IN PLAIN SIGHT HIDDEN

Finally putting out the awning

Friends greet one another

Planning breakfast in the morning

Dogs romp while owners hover

Chairs gather round the fire pit

Pull one up and chat a bit

We share stories of the road

Meet new friends and greet the old

Where'd you come from?

Where are you going?

What kind of dog is that?

Is your water flowing?

Snatches of conversation

Admiring site decorations

Potluck dinners

Cheers and beers

IN PLAIN SIGHT HIDDEN

Playing cards or crafting

Puzzles, hiking, laughing

But it's not all about the blue beret

Even amid all our play

A local charity will benefit

From rally fees Airstreamers pay

Community beyond the road

Helping others bear their load

It's the journey that matters most

As Wally Byam said

But friends along the byways

Brighten the path ahead

See more, do more, live more

Let the rocking chair wait

Travel in an Airstream

You'll lose track of the date

IN PLAIN SIGHT HIDDEN

As you drive over the next hill and the next

Wheels turn and axles flex

No worries about being late

Your traveling home offers rest

At any time while adventure awaits

Whether old or new, towed or driven

There's joy in the wandering; it's a given

As part of a caravan

Or without any plan

There's nothing like Airstream living

May your path be smooth

And your life be blessed

With Airstream friends

In all your treks

BALLOON FIESTA IN SILVER

One of the most highly sought-after Airstream rallies takes place each year at the International Balloon Fiesta in Albuquerque, New Mexico. The Fiesta hosts many RVs overnight at Balloon Fiesta Park. Lined up at the edge of the huge field where hundreds of balloons assemble for flight, Airstreamers enjoy front row seats and the occasional flight of balloons soaring above their rigs.

Breath of giants hissing, sighing

Wakens me at dawn

I leap out of my Airstream

Settle my chair on the lawn

Glowing spheres take shape

Rising from the earth

Tethered by hands and lines grown small

Under burgeoning bright girth

At last the signal's given

They rise into the air

Spiraling and drifting

IN PLAIN SIGHT HIDDEN

In rows but not too near

Such perilous kissing

Would send them crashing down to earth

Instead they fly alone

In formations fluid, shifting

Far beneath their glowing flight

Dogs bark and look about, whining

At what they hear outside their sight

Above them in the dawn's near night

Barely seen, then suddenly bright, shining

Patterns play

Reflections from globes glowing bright

On the silver skin of my Airstream

Black windows capture ribbons of light

As far above tongues of flame sprout

And warm the air inside

IN PLAIN SIGHT HIDDEN

Expanding nylon envelopes

Giant lungs cannot exhale

Until time comes to turn tail

And seek again the gentle slopes

Far below their invisible trail

Some ride breezes back to their fans

Others must be chased by vans

Whether near or far they must land

Be deflated, wrapped, resigned

Sheets of colors, patterns, now ropes bind

Stuffed into protective bags confined

So brief and yet so marvelous

Mighty and so frail

To soar above the RVs

And on air currents sail

Like dreams and fantasies

Until we startle, awake

IN PLAIN SIGHT HIDDEN

Grasping baskets, lines

Gloved hands, knees scraped

Yet for the glory of flight

The crews will do it all again

The very next morning

They'll rise early to ascend

Propane heaters roaring

Bright glowing globes soaring

Riding currents in the air

Circling over the valley

Delighting Albuquerque

Momentary masters of the sky

Until once more home to earth they fly

TOMATOES AND TORNADOES

I often stay at Boondockers Welcome locations when I travel in my Airstream. These sites, accessible for an annual membership fee, are at the homes of other people who travel in RVs. Frequently, I enjoy getting to know my hosts. This experience stands out as an example of a very kind host in unexpected circumstances.

Softly the rain prances

with tiny droplets dances

on my tin roof

Lulling me softly to sleep

A siren and knock on the door

send me stumbling out in the morn

To shelter in a house much more

Solid and suited for a storm

Face unwashed, sleepy eyes

I settle into a chair

IN PLAIN SIGHT HIDDEN

Check the dark yellow skies

Wonder if a twister's near

Outside fierce downpours streaming

Twisted branches turn and sway

A faint siren is screaming

But the merled dog wants to play

Distracted from thunder by balls and toys

The pup fearlessly bounds through the room

The storm recedes to a faint sighing noise

Sunlight begins to pierce the dim gloom

Scrambled eggs with tomatoes

A delightful surprise

Prepared by my host

As the storm subsides

I thank the kind cook and offer grace

With an extra soft prayer

IN PLAIN SIGHT HIDDEN

Praising God for the food and this place

And not least for His care

Back in my Airstream the rain softly beats

A melody lulling me back to sleep

Soothing my soul as I sit and sip

Bittersweet coffee…drip, drip, drip

I relax and think of how much more

Than anything else I choose you Lord

Love you and thank you, praise and adore

Drawing me closer, yourself outpoured

Wherever I am I know you are there

In your light I find I'm home anywhere

Softly the rain prances

With tiny droplets dances

On my tin roof

FIRESIDE

Fellowship and camaraderie by the fire nourish many a friendship on the road. Yet some of what I cherish most about campfires are after everyone else retires for the night and I remain to watch the fire die.

The embers glow red in the night

as small puffs of frozen breath filter from our mouths

the stars above

diamond bright

clear in a dark sky

with drifting dark clouds tinted with purple and blue

now barely seen

stained by the faint remnants of the sun

that just slipped beneath the edge of the world

dimmed

Like remnants of the bright fire

where people gathered round

laughing, drinking, roasting soft puffs of white on sticks

until charred black splitting

or delicate brown crisping

dripping sweet warm cream within

The glowing circle is now quiet and silent

Just me sitting in the dark

with my bucket of water and a stick to poke the embers

I could douse the glowing red coals

but I gaze at them instead and soak in the sounds of night

knowing you are near

and that I share these moments with you

simply sitting,

being,

living,

breathing,

loving what you have made

Over my head stars slowly stroll across the sky

as the glowing embers fade

IN PLAIN SIGHT HIDDEN

leaving soft gray ash behind in shapes echoing

the wood and coal consumed

in the morning those shadow remnants will collapse

and fall into the soft sand mingling

yet even then

behind the bright blue sky, the sun, the clouds

the silent stars remain

Like my memories of stories shared

friends gifted, glasses clinked and lifted

Prayers offered

and you

always there

in the light or darkness

with me

STORMS AND INNER PEACE

When I'm camping, it is not uncommon to find myself being rocked in the middle of the night by the wind as I sleep in my Airstream. Of course, I keep my weather app on in case it is more wind than I want to ride out in my trailer!

The wind howls and pries and spits

In vain it tries to lift

but merely rocks my little ship

I close my eyes and listen

I know I'm safe within

Held softly in a silver cradle

that's riveted not riven

Sheltered in your arms

my many faults forgiven

Still, I'm glad my home is hitched

to that sturdy truck in front

and all the stabilizers down

Curved corners of my castle blunt

The pressure of the gale

IN PLAIN SIGHT HIDDEN

that passes, cannot get a grip

on my shiny silver whale

Over its curves the storm will slip

away into the night

leaving me beyond its grasp

hidden, safe, out of sight

My tin boat on land

lies within your hand

I need not fear outside

But in your peace subside

For all things you provide

And I in love abide

Here in my silver cradle

That gently rocks most stable

 Both storm and sun allied

To lead me near to you

To wander in your ways

To ponder endless days

IN PLAIN SIGHT HIDDEN

The mystery of you

How love and sacrifice renew

Make straight again what's skewed

And so

I skip, I dance on tip toes

Trusting if I fail

You'll catch me still and yet again

Place me on the trail

To follow ever after

Until I reach the top

Where you'll be waiting for me

Where dancing shall not stop

PART THREE: IDENTITY

THE GARDENER

The parable of the seeds in part inspired me to write this poem. Thinking about the hard-packed path, I imagined it as clay and the rocky ground as sand, all of which like the rich soil benefit from the gardener's cultivation. The thorns were withered by trust in the gardener and did not even get their own verse.
The rest of the inspiration for this poem came from an outdoor farmer's market. Colorful fresh vegetables and fruit, including avocados three times the size of those I purchase in the supermarket, prompted musings on their source.

    I till the dark soil

    rich rising scent

    Ripe and pregnant

    With all that may

    Emerge from what is sown

    Scattered expectations thrown

    I till the red clay

    Chopping clumps with sharp cuts

    Adding black humus

    Pulling out stones

IN PLAIN SIGHT HIDDEN

Crunching clods into dust

So that infant rhizomes

May grow, spread, thrust

Through newly soft loam

Piercing broken crust

I till the sandy soil

Mix in rich compost

hard grains cut with softness

Creating with my toil

Culture ready to nourish

Seeds sown in new earth

Dirt scored in furrows

Prepared for new birth

Grains sprout

pushing earth away

Tendrils reach up to the light

With spreading leaves and stems

IN PLAIN SIGHT HIDDEN

And down with hollow roots to soak in waters

Seeping underneath, rising from the depths

To anchor those who seek

To bloom, to later offer gifts of fruit so sweet

Rich colors, bursting flavors,

juice dribbling down our cheeks

Divine Gardener

Grant that I may

Grow in your soil here

Till my soul

That seeds may flourish there

New growth reaching up to you

Rooted in your grace

Nourished by prayer

May I bear

Good fruit, produce to share

Make of me a rich harvest

The work of your hands

IN PLAIN SIGHT HIDDEN

And most sacred Heart

Give me a small part

In your great plans.

Let me lead others to you

to satisfy hunger and thirst

To offer to the gardener

first fruits most choice

And when you harvest what you sowed in this place

Bring me home too, uprooted but safe

Until at last I may gaze on your Face

In the great Feast that never ends

Rejoicing with you, our family and friends.

A GENTLE CONVERSATION ON MY DRIVE NORTH

I wrote this poem by the side of a winding road in Montana, struck by the beauty of my surroundings. A version of it appeared in my first book, Journeys with a Tin Can Pilgrim: from corporate lawyer to Airstream nomad, finding joy in everyday life.

As I drive the winding, climbing, descending roads

Marvels unfold at every turn at every curve

Far away plains and mountains

Trees sheltering rippling streams

A piercing bolt of purple flowers swaying in the breeze

Vast golden fields of yellow blooms

Swaths of deep green fir trees like dark ribbons

adorning the bronze-tipped grass hills

I love you, He says to me

Each delight I would have made just for you

As I died for you

and would have done if you were the only one I created

IN PLAIN SIGHT HIDDEN

His love is so generous and expansive

Like a mother who loves each of her children

There is no limit on that love

The more children the more love

He sees us each

He is fascinated with the smallest details of our days,

our humble sweet gifts clumsily made that we bring to Him

delight Him,

as the scribbles of a small child delight his parents

who hang art on the refrigerator door

Here, my beloved God, is my poem, my photo, my prose,

my feeble but heartfelt praise,

my return to you in small measure

of what you give in great abundance

Each bit of beauty is a caress, a kiss,

an embrace by the white clouds,

IN PLAIN SIGHT HIDDEN

by the snow on the mountains, even by the shadows

as swiftly moving clouds play hide and seek

with the sun beams on the hills

He gives this to me

I praise Him and adore Him and bless Him

in thankfulness and amazement.

I wish to share it with you,

but I am the recipient not the Giver.

Still, I long to pass this to you, my friends,

brothers, sisters, children, fellow travelers.

May I share this sense of His delight,

of utter abandonment in love?

Can I help you open your heart to this gift,

to God's ever-present, glorious,

all-encompassing Love?

Like another dimension, present but unseen,

IN PLAIN SIGHT HIDDEN

we glimpse it from the edges of our eyes,

our hands reach,

our bodies breath in deeply

the scent of roses and pine on the wind,

as we listen to the silence.

Only He can give this to you and He does.

Receive it, dear ones, because you are dear to Him.

In knowing Him, loving Him,

we know and love ourselves and others

and all He has created.

FRIENDS NOW AND FOREVER

One of my friends was fighting a long battle with cancer when I wrote this poem for her. She is a beautiful soul who inspires me with her grace and faith. Although she passed recently into eternity, I know we will meet again.

She glows

She cries

She places eyelashes around her eyes

Her head now smooth

She wraps in cloth

With swirls of color like a butterfly or moth

Whose gorgeous wings have unfurled

She metamorphosizes

on paths unknown, unanticipated

Something new, recreated

Life beyond what metastasizes

She gathers beauty like a cloak

With patterns decorated

Yet she wears that beauty from within

That only comes from life in Him

It shines through her eyes

In her smile, brilliant white

Sometimes

She breathes small sighs

grows weary of her fight

Yet turns again to you, Her Lord

with a litany of trust and praise

repeated through the darker days

Her prayer her sword

She battles on

Seizing life yet sees the rest

Knowing she is truly blest

IN PLAIN SIGHT HIDDEN

Her joy undimmed sheds light for those

She touches on her way

With whistling, singing, laughter

Cherishing each day

As she will in the hereafter

Meet us on our way

With whistling, singing, laughter

In endless bright array

SPIRITUAL CHILDHOOD

This poem is about our identities as beloved children of God. A version appeared in my first book, Journeys with a Tin Can Pilgrim: from corporate lawyer to Airstream nomad, finding joy in everyday life. *There, I used it to illustrate the creativity that develops along the road. Here, I include it as a reflection of who we truly are.*

After that crazy, intense, falling in love time of life

When it is quiet and peaceful,

It is easy to take you for granted,

to crowd you out with things that I must do,

with events that seem important.

Let me see what is important through your eyes,

not mine.

I drift away, careless child wandering down the shore

building sand castles to cry when they collapse

Running after the glitter of bright shells,

translucent pale yellow and orange

IN PLAIN SIGHT HIDDEN

catching the sun,

or so it seems…

Yet I ignore the sun burning me

or the waves that creep under my feet

sucking away the sand with an inhalation

then spitting me out.

Falling back into your arms, you scoop me up, dry my tears,

brush away the sand, heal the stings.

I rest, wrapped in a towel, in your strong arms,

my head on your shoulder under the umbrella.

And, there's ice cream, cool and sweet,

turning my sticky tears into sticky hands

that you cover with kisses.

I rest in you, lulled by the waves and breezes,

the cries of gulls and sounds of children playing,

IN PLAIN SIGHT HIDDEN

as I gaze enraptured at the whorls of a shell

you placed in my grubby hands.

There, within the endless concentric swirls

of peach and cream,

hidden under the rough knobbed surface, I stay silent

until my tired eyes close

and I dream

secure in your love.

YOUR DWELLING PLACE

Another take on identity in relationship with God and one another.

Dwell in me, Lord

Let me be swept away

In the waters flowing forth from your temple, from your side

Let me soak in your peace

Swim in endless seas

It's all love, just being with you

Drinking in that deep

Tasting contentment and happiness

Filled with joy I cannot speak

I see you in

A mother cradling her sleepy child

Soothing with her touch and presence

limbs droop, eyes close, by love beguiled

IN PLAIN SIGHT HIDDEN

I see you in

A father lifting up a child on his shoulders

Humbling himself to carry his small rider

Whose arms are thrown wide in delight

Eyes wider as if awake he dreamed

Raised high by father's gentle might

Caught again if fallen, by love redeemed

I see you yet again within

A nurse wiping a patient's brow with a cool cloth

Sisters smiling and singing to you in chorus

Dancers who leap and twirl

Offering their joy

Despite the pain

of scrunched toes, sore throats, aching feet

Refreshed by living water sweet

I see you again in

an elderly couple, wrinkled hands entwined

IN PLAIN SIGHT HIDDEN

Sitting silently on a bench together

No words remain, by love refined

And once more I see you in

the glowing sunset, a flowing river,

Hidden in mossy trees

in the whistle of birds

and the rustle of leaves

All creation sings your glory

Glows

In your reflected light

In stone churches in silent adoration

Falling to our knees

Having consumed you, now dwelling with you

You within and still above

On the altar shining

Exposed in brightness and in love

IN PLAIN SIGHT HIDDEN

I enraptured in my pew

Caught up, all thoughts inclining

In this moment towards you climbing

As we all, everywhere, at once breathe

As Heaven touches Earth aligning

In this moment, hour, eternally finding

Vistas of rippling grass rising to panoplies of stars

Wave tossed seas gentled like glass

A still small wind softly sighing

Mirroring your beauty wild

Timeless, ceaseless, unending God

I praise thee

Almighty beloved

Stooping down to embrace me

Lifted on your shoulders, your child

PART FOUR: GOD

BY THE SIDE OF THE RIVER

As I hike, I try to take time to sit and be still, to listen to the sounds of nature. Sometimes closing my eyes helps. These moments often turn into prayer as I listen for the quiet voice of God in the lazy humming of insects and the warmth of the sun on my face.

Give this time to me

No one else

Rest in my peace

The water flows past fallen trees, drifting logs

Soft sound of ripples and eddies

swirling in streams that join the flow

I AM

here in your heart

You are

my tabernacle

as I live in your soul, your mind, your heart

IN PLAIN SIGHT HIDDEN

Nothing can separate us

but much can distract you from Me

You always have My full attention

whether you slow down to set a while and talk

or not

Dear child, your thoughts dance

like dragonflies on the water

Go beneath the surface to the stillness

I am there

WALKING WITH JESUS AT THE SHORE

I wrote this poem while hiking along a deserted beach in winter. I'd just returned from Mass and was meditating upon the mystery of the Eucharist.

Pebbles come and go

Rolling along the shore

Rocks once dropped into flowing waters

become smooth and small.

Dams burst, rivers flood

I cannot be contained.

I am not trapped in a box.

I humbly enter in, into humanity,

then into the very substance of food and drink,

bread and wine, transforming it into myself

so you may be with me most intimately.

IN PLAIN SIGHT HIDDEN

The rocks that melt are the obstacles,

the hardness of heart

that I, the living water, wear away

uncovering the gems inside,

the light given to you that you may become light in Me.

The dancing reflections on the surface,

the glow of sunshine piercing into the deep:

it is all there to see

for those who open their eyes and their hearts to Me.

I gather you in, into My heart, dear children.

WITH MY FRIEND IN PRAYER AND WORK

Prayer is a conversation with God. He is our Creator, our Lover, and our best friend. When you spend time with Him each day, even in the middle of being occupied with many things, He multiplies your time and enriches your day with His companionship.

    Come away by yourself to a quiet place

    Close your eyes

    Take a deep breath filling your lungs with sweet air

    Exhale…draw breath in again

    Know that I am with you

    The one who loves you

    Who has all things in mind and in hand

    Hello my dear one

    Tell me about your day

    What worries you, what troubles do you face

    Give them to me

IN PLAIN SIGHT HIDDEN

I will never leave you to walk alone

Always I surround you

and so do your other friends,

even those beyond your sight or touch

An invisible network lifts you up

in love

Like the glorious weaving of a spiderweb

that you pass unseen

When dew falls or sunlight strikes,

it reveals its beauty for a moment,

disappearing quickly from outer sight

yet still present

when you search and seek it with your heart, longing

I created it all

And you too – especially you –

with whom I share a unique relationship as I do

with each child I marvelously and wonderfully made.

IN PLAIN SIGHT HIDDEN

Uniquely you and uniquely them,

together with all in communion, in community,

like Me -- Father, Son, and Holy Spirit --

One Trinity.

One Love, everlasting and ever present,

within which you are the you I formed to be loved.

And you – yes, you -- are invited

to enter into that communion

with Me and all others in my Love.

Here's a small step, my dear – just sit here a while with Me.

Tell me about your day.

Then listen.

Listen for an answer to your questions,

in the gentle breeze,

the scent of dandelions and grass,

the soft rustle of leaves above,

IN PLAIN SIGHT HIDDEN

the scrambling of squirrels,

the varied voices from feathered throats

Listen for me in the voices of others,

in holy Scripture,

in what catches your eye

just out of sight, unperceived

before you truly looked

My voice always leaves you with peace

even when I don't tell you what you think you want to hear

Those quiet times of prayer, of sitting still with me,

will stay with you still

Even as you grasp a seatback in a swaying train

crowded with grumpy commuters,

go through your notes before stepping up to a podium,

or prepare a meal

while folding laundry,

answering your children's questions,

and feeding your dog — all at the same time.

You can touch that peace and listen

To my voice in your heart

the better part

in the middle of the busy world.

PART FIVE: PRAYER

A PILGRIM'S PRAYER

At the end of Mass, we often hear the dismissal "Go in peace, glorifying the Lord with your life." What does this charge mean for me? How do I glorify God with my life?

Lord, let me not be or seek to be the center of attention.

You are the center.

Let all I do point to you, reveal you, adore you, glorify you.

Save me from my own pride,

from seeking comfort and praise,

from anything you do not will for me.

Let me be united to you in perfect love.

Let your peace given to me

draw others to you,

through me

if that is your will.

IN PLAIN SIGHT HIDDEN

Let me scatter the seeds you sow

that you may reap.

Amen.

A PRAYER FOR TRUST

Sometimes I feel down and wonder whether anything I'm doing makes sense or has value. I get discouraged at perceived setbacks. Then, God reminds me that He is with me and gently chides me for my lack of trust and my demand for understanding. Reason and faith exist together, but trust and hope are what binds them as a firm foundation.

Lord, let me offer no resistance to you

Let me, I beg you,

conform myself to your love

To all that you wish to do in me and through me

You are beautiful, my little one

I made you so

All the sorrows and pain of this life

are simply chipping away at the shell

That separates you from me fully

Lord, let me listen with my whole heart

and mind and soul

IN PLAIN SIGHT HIDDEN

Keeping still

That I may hear you

Stop worrying

Pray, hope and trust me

You will hear what you need to hear

when you need to hear it

What I want

is your sacrifice of love and trust

that you are in my hands fully and willingly

no matter whether it makes sense to you

or you can't figure it out

Trust my love

I will nothing bad,

nothing to harm you

Only to shape you

to uncover the You that I made in joy and love

ALL FOR LOVE

It speaks for itself! No explanation is needed for those who love.

God Creator of all

May you accept my offering to you

Of myself, of my all

Giving back to you

What you gave to me

Choosing you

Over all

God, Beloved of my heart

May I follow you closely

Rejoicing always in your will

Knowing what you want

Is perfect beyond all my imaginings

I will to rest in your will

IN PLAIN SIGHT HIDDEN

God, Redeemer of all things

Who loves the world and all within

Who found us very good

In your great goodness

Who gives us life, gives us growth, gives

us your Son, your Spirit, your Self

May I

Accept all your gifts

And become one to others for you

Amen

ABOUT THE AUTHOR

Several years ago, author Lynda Rozell sold her house, quit her job, and embarked on life as a full-time RV nomad. She now lives in a 19-ft Airstream travel trailer that she tows with a RAM 1500 truck. Since becoming a nomad, Lynda writes, performs her poetry, and speaks about RV travel topics, ranging from dealing with bad weather to finding campsites and safety for the solo traveler. She also offers presentations on finding your purpose in life, trusting God, detachment and downsizing, prayer life, and pilgrimage sites. Her travel blog, www.tincanpilgrim.com, shares reflections about travel, particularly the religious sites, shrines, and areas of natural beauty she visits.

RECENT PUBLICATIONS

Lynda's travel memoir, *Journeys with a Tin Can Pilgrim: from corporate lawyer to Airstream nomad, finding joy in everyday life*, chronicles her transformation from her previous life as a lawyer to that of a Tin Can Pilgrim. Published in 2021 by St. John's Press, the book provides everything you need to know about how to live or travel in an RV, based on Lynda's adventures. Through engaging stories, Lynda invites others into the communities she finds on the road and to grow in relationship with God. Her book is available on Amazon at https://www.amazon.com/dp/B09YJN5WTK or at your local bookstore.

PHOTOGRAPHY

All photographs used in the book were taken by Lynda Rozell at locations she visited in her Airstream travels.